A Look At Life

A Look At Life

Written by:
Jeremy Troy Donald Mello

Charleston, SC
www.PalmettoPublishing.com

A Look At Life

First Edition

Paperback ISBN: 978-1-63837-746-7
Hardcover ISBN: 978-1-63837-747-4

Life Quotes From An Ancient Soul

Keep your cup full never overflowing
unless it waters those you love.

◊◊

Be like fruit; both sweet and nutritious,
clean and free, protective but generous.

◊◊

Learn who in actuality you are, instead
of who you believe you are. This is when
you can perform at your highest.

◊◊

Good goes well with piety.

People like to say that it is a small world, but that is because they do not go many different places. When really it is a big world ready for exploration.

◊◊

Hate can be real, but the real is much realer.

◊◊

Some people do a whole lot of nothing while doing something, a better goal, rather, would be to do a whole lot of something while doing little.

Try not to ruminate over things that do not largely affect your reality.

◊◊

Hate is a miserable emotion, there isn't much winning that goes on with hating.

◊◊

We are in the Universe, the uni-verse is the unification of everything connected by love. Love is respect, while respect the start of love.

Being patient is being God's patient, wait and be healed.

◊◊

Compare what is true to what is fake so then you won't get confused.

◊◊

It is love or it is justice. Choose love.

◊◊

Words form ideas if the ideas are different use different words.

The best gift to give is genuine love.

◊◊

When people stop doing good, that is unfortunate for them, but when people then try and stop other people from doing good, justice must come.

◊◊

There is not much competition if you level up independently.

Without rules, there isn't a game, without laws there isn't life, if not human, natural, if not natural Godly.

◊◊

If you live like there is no right and wrong in life you have shown that you have given up in life, for to better your being is to build on what is just, this strengthens your character.

People who win in life do not try too much. They give their top effort and are satisfied.

◊◊

Those who think that mimicking something gives off the same affect as genuine expression are mistaken.

◊◊

Authenticity is where you find truth and a strong hold, whereas foolery is frail and will eventually unravel.

Those who treat others based on how others treat them instead of being compassionate to all should be sure to show accurate first impressions. If not, then others could be doing the same and that would be contradictory to that approach.

◊◊

Study is learning. Science sometimes has too much curiosity for its own good.

Extending our vocabulary is to better communicate our emotional energy.

◊◊

Little things can turn into big things. Although it may be cliché, it is always good to try and do your best.

◊◊

Life is a test to prove your loyalty to God. Also, to yourself and your loved ones.

Justice goes higher than human law. This is why it should be lived not only enforced.

◊◊

GOD, and your devotion to the divine should always come first.

◊◊

They often say to believe in yourself, but beliefs many times hold lies. Self-confidence is knowing your worth and what you are capable of. And trust and faith can bring you even higher.

Remember that there is not a change in the quality of work whether it has been materialistically rewarded or not. Recognize the value of the work rather than the payment.

◊◊

The Eleven Virtues to Life:
Truthfulness, Respect, Responsibility, Prudence, Justice, Love, Self-Control, Fortitude, Naturality, Patience and Trust in GOD; Source; Divinity

Those who know they are in the wrong and continue to fight only worsen their outcome. While admitting the defeat is a possible path to redemption, persisting might increase the consequence.

◊◊

Luck is but favor from the Divine.

Contrary to common belief, sacrificing yourself for others is not a virtue when assisting them, especially if it can be helped. Caring for yourself enough to help others without damaging yourself in the process brings a mutual benefit for everybody.

◊◊

Those who only see success in a material type of way are far from knowing what success really is.

Treating life like a game and then playing without rules defeats its own purpose. Ultimately life is sacred, and we should treat it as such.

◊◊

Belittling somebody for no good reason might lead them to showing you how big they really are.

◊◊

The past influences the future, but the present is the most powerful of moments.

Strong principles and values build a strong life.

◊◊

"Flaws" that complement you are better than perfection. Perfection is an illusion. Just work on being a better you, and it will help you let go of this misleading stigma.

◊◊

When you love, you must leave at least some of yourself vulnerable.
If not, is it really love?

Battle when it is time to battle,
Eat when it is time to eat,
Love when it is time to love,
Do what you need to do for your growth and fulfillment.

◊◊

Sunshine is nice; everybody loves the sunshine. But when you can learn to love the rain, in the storms of life, then you know happiness.

If you do something good without knowing and then you realize it later - this here, is a sign of the guidance from above.

◊◊

In simple terms, everybody decides their own fate. Everybody chooses who they want to be, which makes everybody responsible for how they live. Who you are is who you choose to be (with the exception of what you were born into).

Give up in a way to where your blessings come from, but don't quit so you can earn what you deserve.

◊◊

Everybody sees you differently; what is important is how you see yourself.

◊◊

Abundance often brings wastefulness, but struggle helps you learn how much is necessary.

It's better to be in debt to a bank than to several different people at once.

◊◊

Your people should always come before your money. Place the invaluable above the valuable; what is priceless ahead of what is priced.

◊◊

I do not ask for an easy life; I ask to develop the strength to live a difficult life easily.

Some scars are too deep for it to go back to the way it was. That is why it is important to know when it is time to leave.

◊◊

Always wait for the credit of your own work to reach you; never take the credit of others instead because you might lose the opportunity for your own.

◊◊

It is unwise to trust anybody fully, place this trust in GOD instead.

I feel good when there is chaos,

I feel good when there is peace.

This goodness comes from the love

for life.

◊◊

Great people find truth at the level that

they live their own truth.

◊◊

There is no I am you and you are me.

We are all our own unique manifestation.

Rejoice in similarities but own what is

you and different.

Motion helps shape the physical.
The ocean soothes emotions.
Technology is a tool for each mind.
The right food nourishes our being.
And Nature uplifts the Spirit.

◊◊

Some people love the work that they do. This is what we want.

◊◊

We are co-creators of our lives.
So, we should accept the responsibility for where we are.

Gender is an opposite to know, meant
to be opposite but also meant to be
beautiful when complementing each other.

◊◊

Any substance to escape reality is
unnecessary. We can achieve bliss
or satisfaction within our own life
experiences. Self-work, self-care and
healthy relationships can help us in
attaining these states of being.

"It's all good" should be a dead phrase. It promotes a stagnant attitude instead of motivation and progression towards the solutions to today's problems.

◊◊

Race is sometimes used to be a distraction against unity. Character should be viewed in an individual scope not bunched together as a whole ethnicity.

If you are going to stay on a path, do not choose the path that maintains your image. Instead, choose the path that feeds your potential. This will bring you better results in the long run.

◊◊

Even when you are sick, speak and do things towards healing yourself instead of dwelling on the sickness. This will help steer you to recovery.

The five main attributes to humanistic value: strength, love, beauty, authenticity, and intellect.

◊◊

Keep close the people in your life who accept you for who you truly are. As for those who do not, contemplate removing them.

◊◊

My single rule to my teachings is to acknowledge that there is a Creator of this existence.

Everybody has karma from their past life or the life that they are currently living. Once you live honestly and have paid off most of your karmaic debt, you may start to realize that you now have instant consequence for your wrongdoing. This is not a punishment. This means you are free from your karma since it is not delayed anymore, and you have a clean slate. Most importantly, since you are being taught directly on how to "perfect" your flaws, you can now use this growth to live towards your highest potential.

Knowing how much to give and receive is important for growth.

◊◊

It is always better to have enough than to have too much.

◊◊

I have found the meaning of life; it is to grow.

Remember how big this universe is; we do not only come from this planet, but our makeup also comes from galaxies, from the cosmos and beyond.

◊◊

I myself do not associate winning in life with competition anymore. I see it as conquering the trails that are encountered and the succession of self-improvement.

Be nice because kindness kills; one is courteous while the other can be misleading and self-harming.

◊◊

The feeling of Heaven has been revealed to my being. Its beauty I can feel without sight or sound. The feeling although fleeting, I can never forget its message. The message, as the feeling itself, is to inspire me to discover its completeness.

Everybody wants to win,
but it sometimes seems like nobody
wants to win the right way.

◊◊

Capitalism is motivation for people's contribution to society. Without production competition or motivation or even inspiration, there would be less progress to modernity and innovative production. The view here is through not a monetary accumulating lens but a creativity enhancing one.

(continued)

The downside that I see is the lack of responsibility from the materialistically wealthy. They must cease putting money over living things, and we would have larger success for the whole.

◊◊

Everybody has strengths from which they can derive reward . The tough part is finding what they are and how to use them.

Be careful of those who "love" you
only to get what they want.

◊◊

There is always going to be that hole
of uncertainty; fill it with faith and trust
and continue to do your part.

Hiding from your feelings and not caring is not a promising way to recover from trauma you have been through or recent damage you have taken on.
Feel it, learn from it, and then don't think too much about it in the future. Suppressing emotion is only a temporary fix and it will always somehow find its way out to be expressed.

(continued)

When a volcano erupts, pressure builds
up inside of it and then explodes
causing damage to its surroundings.
Much like this, the emotions that are
suppressed could eventually overflow,
damaging you and those around you.

◊◊

Sometimes it is ok to just exist.

◊◊

Fear can also be a good teacher.

Healthy expression can do wonders.

◊◊

A fully healed heart is harder to break.

◊◊

Lift people's spirits not just weight.

◊◊

View enemies as only an obstacle;
to acknowledge their "greatness" is
degrading your own.

Life is more about self-improvement than it is competition.

◊◊

Too much help sometimes hurts.

◊◊

I once saw copycats looking curious.

◊◊

If people turn your happiness that you share with them into jealousy, no longer share it with them.

Lose expectation; find happiness.

◊◊

The thing about teaching the masses is you're most likely teaching those who are against you too. But to be aware of this is already being steps ahead.

◊◊

It is very difficult to belittle those who know their worth.

There is no matrix. The matrix that they talk about is in their own imprisoned minds. Breakout and be naturally free.

◊◊

A sage can teach all they want, but they know the ultimate victory is when the people find their truth on their own or with little assistance.

◊◊

The reason is not to take credit but more so to make progress.

I have fought for many, suffered for some, and died for none.

◊◊

For financial secureness, an exceptional credit score is more important than money.

◊◊

To live a life of imitation is one of the worst ways to be.

If they take my courage, I'll replace it with bravery. If they take my hope, I'll replace it with faith. If they take my happiness, I'll turn it into bliss.

◊◊

Those who use their own free will against a virtuous cause better not be sobbing when they have to face the consequences.

◊◊

GOD is bigger than any spiritual book.

People often wait for the end; why not wait for a new beginning?

◊◊

Don't be too concerned over the people who point out your mistakes when they have their own mistakes to correct.

◊◊

I went into the dark to take what was mine, then I returned to my light and enjoyed it there.

The essence of life is to love.

◊◊

Be sure not to lose your optimism to ignorance.

◊◊

Use your devotion and life lessons as protection against misfortune.

◊◊

The closer you get to God the easier God will hear you.

Where interest is, passion follows; where passion is, diligence and fulfillment reside.

◊◊

Break your own chain before you try and break others'.

◊◊

See life's tests as motivation. If they are tougher, you are growing higher.

Knowing what you are not lets you know more of what you are.

◊◊

To aspire to be something can be a beautiful thing, but to believe you're something you are not is like living a lie.

◊◊

Truth can hurt, but it is rewarding.

◊◊

The further somebody digs their hole, the tougher it is to get to the top.

Fall in love? No, rise in love.

◊◊

They might doubt my worth, but I can also doubt their judgement.

◊◊

Don't ever base what you do off of what everybody else does. You might be meant for more.

I try not to ask for too much; I try not to give too much, but I don't mind if I live too much

◊◊

They might use your past against you; just be aware of your mistakes. It is cowardice anyway to call somebody out when they are on their way to bettering themselves.

It is right to forgive, but sometimes it does take time to heal. If they are not giving you enough time to heal and continue to wrong you, they should expect some sort of rebuttal or change of attitude.

◊◊

People often make the mistake of blaming divinity for their own faults when it is their responsibility to accept the result of their own actions.

There is a difference between following and chasing people.

◊◊

I saw that I was worthy of love, and for me that was enough.

◊◊

When they often see and mention your flaws, look towards your own budding potential.

You cannot be the best at something by faking it; somebody who is authentic with their purpose will always eventually be greater.

◊◊

Two friends who love you are greater than six friends who like you.

◊◊

The image that should be maintained should not be an image but rather the essence of who you truly are.

Everybody wants to know, but when we embrace the unknown it is much more fun.

◊◊

Life may be a stage and God the director, but there are always auditions before a great play.

◊◊

People might let you down; still choose to go up.

You can go as far as the Universe will let you.

◊◊

Why do they use their time to bring others down when they could be using their time to build themselves up instead.

◊◊

People should be valued who let other people be their true selves without any tension or ridicule.

Too much exaggeration devalues your words.

◊◊

Sometimes when you lose, you still win. Life is like that.

◊◊

There is often more than meets the eye when tragedy happens.

◊◊

Fear is only a shadow; the light will help you see this.

Love comes from the soul first, so there is still hope for the heartless.

◊◊

The Heavens smile upon those who chase their dreams with good intentions.

◊◊

Don't confuse a bribe for a blessing.

I do not promise because I do not know. But what I do know is that people who serve lies and expect fulfilled promises are foolish.

◊◊

It is ok to have a crown that does not fit your head. Keep moving towards prosperity until you have found a place that fits.

Being rich from seeking attention is nothing like being rich from being yourself.

◊◊

Always remember that your presence matters.

◊◊

"The end" is only a new beginning.

Don't let your efforts to make people happy bother you too much. Sometimes it is up to the other person to do their own inner work for their happiness.

◊◊

Learn and live.

◊◊

With closeness to God comes more meaning to your life.

Forcing or manipulating somebody to do what is right for themselves is almost as bad as manipulating somebody to do what is wrong. Although these people might be trying to help, it is possible to help too much, and people have to learn to grow on their own.

◊◊

Good sleep will only strengthen your dreams.

All she wants is the finer things.. but what about the finest things?

◊◊

True love starts as a friend, and then builds into more.

◊◊

Don't ever give your best to somebody undeserving.

Many unseen things hold great value, like knowledge and intelligence, yet many people see value only in the things that can be seen.

◊◊

The best treasures are usually hidden and not easily found.

Listening is a key component to success, especially listening to the words unspoken. I am not only talking about external success but also self-betterment.

◊◊

You could go to companies with money but going where there is good company seems to be more of a solution.

◊◊

They may doubt, but you know what you been through.

Unite and conquer.

◊◊

I still pour the poor the same thing out of my cup.

◊◊

A virtuous warrior always chooses his battles wisely to prevent the war.

◊◊

The truth can kill but is it not the devils that die.

The more honest and true you are to yourself and others the easier it is to find truth.

◊◊

Just remember there is "honey" in the word honesty.

◊◊

There are people who address other people with slandering names and then they wonder where the respect is.

Beautiful people belong in beautiful places.

◊◊

What is knowledge without wisdom or good judgement.

◊◊

Invest in what is benefiting you. Try to find mutual types of exchanges.

I have felt like the world has been against me, and I have felt like the world has been rigged in my favor. I have disliked both of these feelings.

◊◊

If I share love with you, share it with others.

◊◊

Evil is there to show you what not to do.

Learn the difference between connection and attachment. Relationships are much stronger not being attached to each other but rather being well connected.

◊◊

It is not about the money as much as it is about the work.

It was to be or not to be. It was everything or not anything at all. So, we must choose wisely what we do with this everything.

◊◊

If you happen to break into pieces, make your pieces into master-pieces.

◊◊

To make sure your wins are bigger than your losses is to ensure you have a victorious ending.

I have always liked my halo better than my horns.

◊◊

Acknowledge that when people are at their best they likely will assist others on becoming their best as well.

◊◊

I do not like to burn bridges; I would rather build them.

It is ok to open up but be sure to open up to the right person.

◊◊

Caring for yourself strengthens your ability to care for others, in a loving way, of course, not a selfish one.

◊◊

It is not the skin tone that makes people who they are as much as their thoughts, words, actions, and intentions. When people realize this, they will see no reason for racism.

The sky looks upon many flowers, but
the flowers see only one sky.

◊◊

Love without fear.

◊◊

Money earned and used in an honest
way is not only good for the economy
but also good to keep partnerships.

You can repair the outside as much as you like, but it is the inner work that will give you the most reward.

◊◊

Everybody lives and creates their own story; it is not just one being's story, but everybody's story combined that we live and experience.

◊◊

Trust is very important in any relationship especially with GOD and with how everything interconnects.

Know the difference between always wanting more and always wanting to better yourself.

◊◊

There could have been multiple things that happened in an experience but there could always be that one important reason that gets you to a better place in life.

A good question to ask is: do they love you or do they love the money that you have?

◊◊

Some people don't like change, but change is how you can grow into something better.

◊◊

If you fall, learn why you fell.

Most of the pain that people feel is because they go against their own truth. Whether it be positive pain or negative pain, it is there to help you become the best version of yourself.

◊◊

It is ok not to show your whole self to some people. Like anything, some people deserve some things more than others.

◊◊

You know it is bad when people want to see you lose more than themselves win.

Your lows often help you get to your highs.

◊◊

Do not be bitter, but instead get better.

◊◊

There is more value in being a real person than there is in wearing real jewelry.

Everybody wants to be loved, for we are made of love. You have love within you, ready to give and ready to receive. GOD is love and more; it is the top currency of the universe.

◊◊

Love does not hurt; if it hurts, it was not love.

◊◊

Time is not money; time is more valuable.

What is right for one person is not always right for the next.

◊◊

I am without attachment, yet I still stay in touch.

◊◊

Do not be afraid to be alone. Learn the beauty of solitude. There are times for solitude and there are times to spend with friends. One brings peace and the other good conversation.

People call them broke when they do not have any money, as if that determines how strong they are.

◊◊

If you made a relationship into a game, that was your first mistake.

◊◊

Truth is the kind of pain you need.

◊◊

Words from a jealous heart are usually lies.

The upward struggle is only getting you better and remember that the rewards are that much sweeter.

◊◊

Understand that I overstand. But it is understandable if it is tough to understand me.

◊◊

My age is what it is, but my soul is timeless.

It is not about the money; it is about the people.

◊◊

If they put who you are in a box, break through every time.

◊◊

Give out of love and reject bribery.

◊◊

The amazing thought about living in an infinite universe is that nothing is really something.

How you feel is often based upon how you think. If you are thinking positively, it can reflect positive feelings; happy thoughts attract happy times.

◊◊

Eye sea beauty.

◊◊

Contentment is a palace of its own.

◊◊

I might lead sometimes but what I do know is that I follow the truth.

Always choose self-confidence over arrogance. These should not be mistaken.

◊◊

Sometimes you have to go through the darkness to find the light but if you do don't get lost.

◊◊

Always hear both sides of the story before making a conclusion.

It is ok to want what you deserve. But the execution often needs patience and consistency.

◊◊

I can does not always mean I should.

◊◊

It requires practice to get your thoughts aligned with your feelings, but it is better to master your mind than to neglect it.

◊◊

Why trade your happiness for revenge?

Children should learn not because they are forced to but because they want and choose to in their own interest.

◊◊

They showed me the devil, so I showed them the rebel.

◊◊

Excess of freedom is amongst the highest of valuables.

◊◊

Do to become

Following obsessions can lead to problems and discomfort.

◊◊

Communication is key.

◊◊

Some victories are difficult; some are easy but either way we celebrate.

11 Virtues to Life

Truthfulness – Honesty; True to self

Respect - Civility

Responsibility – Accountability

Prudence – Wise judgement

Justice – Knowing right from wrong and when to give or take away

Love – The essence of life

Self-Control - Temperance; Control of self

Fortitude – Courage; Bravery

Naturality – Natural in character; Real; Authentic

Patience – Knowing when and how to wait

TRUST in GOD; Source; Divinity

Three additional virtues for women

Beauty, nurture and faithfulness

11 Types of Love

♡ White – Pure love or self-love, Philautia (Greek), love of self

♥ Black - Business love

♥ Gray – Sad love; Sympathy

♥ Blue – Godly love

♥ Pink – Goddess love

♥ Violet – Divine love

♥ Yellow – Happiness love or Philia (Greek), friendship and affection

♥ Orange – Sexual love; Eros and Ludus (Greek), desirable and playful love

- Green – Love for Nature
- Brown – Nourishing love; Pragma or Storge (Greek), enduring or family love
- Red – A-sexual love; Agape (Greek), charitable love, compassion, romantic love

The Five Main Attributes to Increase Humanistic Value

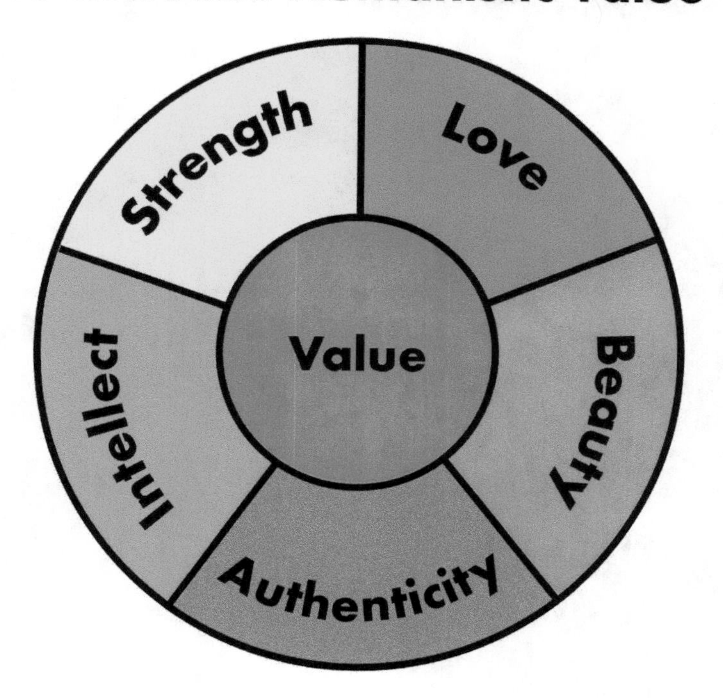

Footprints

If you are lost, look for the footprints in the sand, but don't get distracted because soon they will vanish with the tide.

They may lead you to the water where voyagers have discovered unknown land and where fisherman fish to feed their families.

But then the footprints might stop (from the next on coming wave).

Still. . .I tell you to not get dismayed. . .

Because this is a sign that you are no longer lost but rather on your way. And suddenly you will realize that I was with you all along.

-Jeremy Troy Donald Mello

CPSIA information can be obtained
at www.ICGtesting.com
Printed in the USA
BVHW051123130723
667186BV00010B/870